The Guide to Cooking Tofu

The Ultimate Tofu Cookbook That You Will Ever Need

By

Martha Stone

Copyright 2016 Martha Stone

License Notes

No part of this Book can be reproduced in any form or by any means including print, electronic, scanning or photocopying unless prior permission is granted by the author.

All ideas, suggestions and guidelines mentioned here are written for informative purposes. While the author has taken every possible step to ensure accuracy, all readers are advised to follow information at their own risk. The author cannot be held responsible for personal and/or commercial damages in case of misinterpreting and misunderstanding any part of this Book.

About the author

Martha Stone is a chef and also cookbook writer. She was born and raised in Idaho where she spent most of her life growing up. Growing up in the country taught her how to appreciate and also use fresh ingredients in her cooking. This love for using the freshest ingredients turned into a passion for cooking. Martha loves to teach others how to cook and she loves every aspect of cooking from preparing the dish to smelling it cooking and sharing it with friends.

Martha eventually moved to California and met the love of her life. She settled down and has two children. She is a stay at home mom and involves her children in her cooking as much as possible. Martha decided to start writing cookbooks so that she could share her love for food and cooking with everyone else.

Table of Contents

Introduction 7
   The Top Nine Benefits to Eating Tofu 9
Delicious Tofu Recipes 14
   Tofu Style Pumpkin Pie 15
   Tofu Parmigiana 17
   Vietnamese Style Curry Soup 20
   Honey Mustard Style Tofu 23
   Orange and Ginger Smothered Tofu Triangles 28
   Easy Tofu Sandwich Spread 31
   Vegetarian Style Stuffed Peppers 33
   Cheese and Tofu Stuffed Shells 36
   Simple Chocolate Tofu Pie 39
   Tofu Packed Stroganoff 41
   Tofu Style Salad 44
   Savory Tofu Vindaloo 46
   Vegan Style Cheesecake 49
   Savory Agedashi-esque Style Tofu 51
   Tofu Packed Quiche with Broccoli 53
   Tofu Style Keema 56
   Taiwanese Style Fried Tofu 59
   Filling Tofu and Cauliflower Masala 61
   Traditional Pad Thai Noodles 64
   Tofu Style Turkey 67

Tofu Fillet Sandwiches 71

Tofu Style Burgers 74

Easy Braised Tofu 77

Stove Top Style Tofu Chili 79

Conclusion 81

Author's Afterthoughts 82

Introduction

Tofu, while originating in the East, is one of the most popular health foods today. Whether you are looking to lose some weight, prevent cancer, improve your immune system or are looking just to live a healthier lifestyle, then adding tofu to your daily diet may be the best solution for you. Tofu is packed naturally with important proteins, vitamins and minerals that your body needs in order to thrive.

If you are interested in trying out tofu for yourself and have always wanted to enjoy a healthier food source, then this is certainly the book for you. Inside of this book you will find over 25 of the most healthy and nutritious tofu recipes. On top of that you will discover a few of the benefits that comes with eating tofu so you can see how it will benefit you in the long run.

So, what are you waiting for?

Let's get cooking!

The Top Nine Benefits to Eating Tofu

With people becoming more and more aware about the negative effects obesity and excess weight gain can have on the body, many people are turning to more healthy food products to staying health. Tofu has become an increasingly popular food item used today and it is packed with a variety of benefits. In this section, you will learn about those different types of benefits so you can see how it can help you live a healthier lifestyle in the long run.

1. It Can Help Improve Your Heart Health

One of the largest causes of death in all countries today is heart attacks and development of cardiovascular diseases. Whenever you regularly consume tofu on the other hand, it helps to reduce the risk of having a stroke or developing other cardiac diseases. Tofu helps to do this by reducing the amount of cholesterol within the blood stream as well as raising the level of good cholesterol within the body.

2. Helps to Maintain Blood Pressure

There is a compound found in tofu known as bioactive peptides which are naturally within it and that act as natural antioxidants and anti-inflammatories. This can help repair any damaged blood vessels that you may have and it can also help to reduce high blood pressure. When you add tofu into your regular eating regimen you can help protect your heart in the long run.

3. Helps to Prevent Cancer

We all know how terrible cancer can be. It turns out that cancer is one of the largest causes of death worldwide. Tofu is naturally a source of flavonoids which have a long history of preventing cancerous cells from growing. It also helps to hinder the chance of cancer cells from multiply which can help stops its spread right in its tracks.

4. Help to Increase Weight Loss

Tofu naturally has low cholesterol and fat content, which makes it an amazing food to use whenever you are trying to lose weight. Tofu contains peptins that can help prevent fatty acids from depositing within your body. When you add this into your daily diet it can help you lose a few extra pounds in the process.

5. Helps to Prevent Type 2 Diabetes

The low calorie content and low fat content found within tofu helps to make it a perfect choice for those who are currently suffering from diabetes. Tofu can help to reduce insulin resistance within the blood steam and can even help reduce the risk of developing type 2 diabetes greatly. Not only that the high levels of protein within tofu can help to lower and control blood sugar levels and keep them normalized.

6. Help to Slow Down the Aging Process for Your Skin

Not only is tofu incredibly great for your overall health, but it is incredibly good for your skin as well. The natural protein within tofu helps to improve your skin by improving the elasticity in the cells which can help make your skin look incredibly youthful. Not only that it helps to nourish your skin and stop it from aging prematurely.

7. Helps to Improve Overall Bone Health

Tofu is naturally rich in important bone healthy nutrients such as calcium and magnesium, which can go a long way to improve overall bone health. Tofu itself can easily help to boost bone growth in young children and can even help to prevent bone erosion in most adults. This can help prevent irritating bone issues such as rheumatoid arthritis and osteoporosis as you grow older.

8. Help to Improve the Immune System

The immune system is very important is protecting again various foreign bodies and disease to maintain optimal health. Why not boost your immune system by consuming a bit of tofu here and there? Tofu is naturally rich in various proteins and important vitamins and minerals that can go a long way in improving the function of your immune system.

9. Helps to Prevent Hair Loss

Natural human hair comprises of protein that is used to maintain its overall health, volume and overall quality. Tofu is packed with some of these essential proteins that your hair needs such as selenium. If you want to improve your hair quality, just add a touch of tofu to your daily diet.

Delicious Tofu Recipes

Tofu Style Pumpkin Pie

To kick things off we have a delicious pumpkin pie dish that I know you are going to fall in love with. It is a delicious twist on a classic pie recipe that you won't have to feel guilty about enjoying.

Makes: 8 Servings

Total Prep Time: 2 Hours

Ingredients:

- 1, 10.5 Ounce Pack of Tofu, Silk Variety and Drained
- 1, 16 Ounce Can of Pumpkin, Puree
- ¾ Cup of Sugar, White in Color
- ½ tsp. of Salt, For Taste
- 1 tsp. of Cinnamon, Ground Variety
- ½ tsp. of Ginger, Ground Variety
- ¼ tsp. of Cloves, Ground Variety
- 1, 9 Inch Pie Crust, Unbaked Variety

Directions:

1. The first thing that you will want to do is preheat your oven to 450 degrees.

2. While your oven is heating up place your silk tofu, white sugar, dash of salt, ground cinnamon, ginger and ground cloves into a blend. Blend on the highest setting until smooth in consistency. Pour this mixture into your pie crust.

3. Place into your oven to bake for at least 15 minutes.

4. After this time reduce the heat in your oven to 350 degrees. Continue to bake for the next 40 minutes or until fully baked through.

5. Remove from your oven and allow to cool slightly before serving.

Tofu Parmigiana

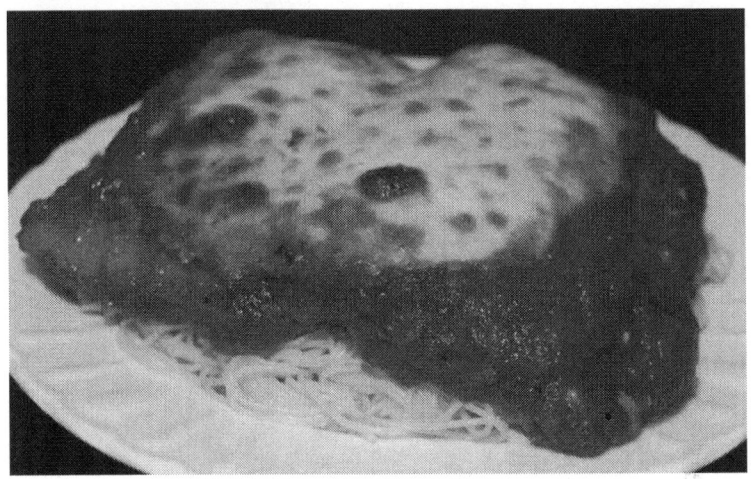

If you are a huge fan of classic Italian dishes, then this is one dish that you need to try for yourself. For the tastiest results serve this dish with some angel hair pasta and garlic bread. Regardless, you are going to love it.

Makes: 4 Servings

Total Prep Time: 45 Minutes

Ingredients:

- ½ Cup of Bread Crumbs, Seasoned Variety
- 5 Tbsp. of Parmesan Cheese, Freshly Grated
- 2 tsp. of Oregano, Evenly Divided
- Dash of Salt, For Taste
- Dash of Black Pepper, For Taste
- 1, 12 Ounce Pack of Tofu, Firm
- 2 Tbsp. of Olive Oil, Extra Virgin Variety
- 1, 8 Ounce Can of Tomato Sauce
- ½ tsp. of Basil, Dried
- 1 Clove of Garlic, Minced
- 4 Ounces of Mozzarella Cheese, Finely Shredded

Directions:

1. Use a small sized bowl and add in your bread crumbs, at least 2 tablespoons of your parmesan cheese, one teaspoon of your oregano and dash of salt and pepper. Stir thoroughly to combine.

2. Next slice your tofu into thick slices. Place into a bowl filled with water. Roll in your bread crumb mixture, making sure to coat thoroughly on all sides.

3. Then heat up some oil in a large sized skillet placed over medium heat. Once your oil is hot enough add in your tofu slices and cook until crispy and brown on all sides.

4. In a small sized bowl add in your tomato sauce, fresh basil, minced garlic and remaining oregano. Stir thoroughly to combine.

5. Place a thin layer of your sauce into a medium sized baking dish. Place your tofu slices on top and top off with your remaining sauce. Top off with some shredded mozzarella cheese and your remaining parmesan cheese.

6. Place into your oven to bake at 400 degrees for the next 20 minutes.

7. Remove after this time and allow to cool slightly before serving.

Vietnamese Style Curry Soup

If you are looking for a great tasting and filling soup to serve up during the cold winter months. This particular dish is seasoned with fresh curry, giving it a hint of spice that you won't be able to resist.

Makes: 8 Servings

Total Prep Time: 2 Hours

Ingredients:

- 2 Tbsp. of Oil, Vegetable Variety
- 1 Onion, Chopped Coarsely
- 2 Shallots, Sliced Thinly
- 2 Cloves of Garlic, Finely Chopped
- 1, 2 Inch Piece of Ginger, Fresh and Sliced Thinly
- 1 Stalk of Lemon Grass, Cut Into Small Sized Pieces
- 4 Tbsp. of Curry, Powdered Variety
- 1 Bell Pepper, Green in Color and Chopped Coarsely
- 2 Carrots, Fresh, Peeled and Sliced
- 8 Mushrooms, Thinly Sliced
- 1 Pound of Tofu, Fried and Cut Into Small Sized Pieces
- 4 Cups of Broth, Vegetable Variety and Homemade Preferable
- 4 Cups of Water, Warm
- 2 Tbsp. of Fish Sauce, Vegetarian Style and Optional
- 2 tsp. of Red Pepper Flakes, For Taste
- 1 Bay Leaf, Fresh
- 8 Potatoes, Small in Size and Cut Into Quarters
- 1, 14 Ounce Can of Milk, Coconut Variety
- 2 Cups of Bean Sprouts, Fresh and For Garnish
- 8 Sprigs of Cilantro, Fresh, Roughly Chopped and For Garnish

Directions:

1. First heat up some oil in a large sized stock pot placed over medium heat. Once your oil is hot enough add in your onions and shallots. Cook until soft to the touch.

2. Add in your garlic, ginger, fresh lemon grass and powdered curry. Cook for another 5 minutes.

3. Then add in your green pepper, fresh carrots, dried mushrooms and fried tofu pieces. Stir to combine and season this mixture with your fish sauce and dash of red pepper flakes.

4. Bring your mixture to a boil before adding in your potatoes and coconut style milk.

5. Once your soup is boiling reduce the heat to low and simmer for at least 40 minutes to an hour or until your potatoes are tender to the touch.

6. Remove from heat and serve. Garnish with your bean sprouts and fresh cilantro.

Honey Mustard Style Tofu

This is a great dish to make if you are looking to satisfy the vegetarian eaters in your household. Packed full of a unique and savory taste, I guarantee your family will be begging for this recipe.

Makes: 4 Servings

Total Prep Time: 45 Minutes

Ingredients:

- 3 Tbsp. of Butter, Soft
- 1 Pound of Tofu, Firm and Sliced Into Thick Slices
- 2 Cups of Flour, Whole Wheat Variety
- 1 Cup of Water, Warm
- ¼ Cup of White Wine, Dried Variety
- 2 Cubes of Bouillon, Vegetable Variety
- 4 Tbsp. of Mustard, Fully Prepared
- ¼ Cup of Honey, Raw

Directions:

1. First melt your butter in a medium sized skillet placed over medium to high heat. Once your butter is fully melted dredge your tofu in some flour and add to your skillet. Cook for the next 10 to 15 minutes or until brown on all sides.

2. After this time add in your water, white wine and vegetable bouillon. Allow your mixture to simmer for the next 10 minutes or until your bouillon fully dissolves.

3. After this time add in your mustard and honey. Stir thoroughly to combine.

4. Continue to simmer until your mixture is thick in consistency.

5. Remove from heat and serve right away.

Healthy Vegetable and Tofu Stir Fry

If you are craving authentic Asian cuisine, then this is the perfect dish for you to make. Smothered in a mouthwatering sauce you won't be able to resist, this dish is certain to please every palate.

Makes: 4 Servings

Total Prep Time: 45 Minutes

Ingredients:

- 1 Tbsp. of Oil, Vegetable Variety
- ½ of an Onion, Medium in Size and Thinly Sliced
- 2 Cloves of Garlic, Chopped Finely
- 1 Tbsp. of Ginger Root, Fresh and Chopped Finely
- 1, 16 Ounce Pack of Tofu, Drained and Cut Into Small Sized Cubes

- ½ Cup of Water, Warm
- 4 Tbsp. of Vinegar, Rice Wine Variety
- 2 Tbsp. of Honey, Raw
- 2 Tbsp. of Soy Sauce, Your Favorite Kind
- 2 tsp. of Cornstarch
- 2 Tbsp. of Water, Warm
- 1 Carrot, Peeled and Thinly Sliced
- 1 Bell Pepper, Green in Color, Seeded and Cut Into Thin Strips
- 1 Cup of Corn, Baby Variety, Drained and Cut Into Small Sized Pieces
- 1 Head of Bok Choy, Small in Size and Roughly Chopped
- 2 Cups of Mushrooms, Fresh and Finely Chopped
- 1 ¼ Cups of Bean Sprouts, Fresh
- 1 Cup of Bamboo Shoots, Drained and Finely Chopped
- ½ tsp. of Red Pepper, Crushed
- 2 Green Onions, Medium in Size and Sliced Thinly

Directions:

1. Use a large sized skillet and heat up some oil over medium to high heat. Once your oil is hot enough add in your onions and cook for at least one minute. Then add in your garlic and ginger. Cook for another 30 seconds.

2. Add in your tofu and cook until golden brown in color.

3. Add in your fresh carrots, green pepper and corn. Stir thoroughly to combine and continue to cook for the next 2 minutes.

4. After this time add in your bok choy, mushrooms, fresh bean sprouts, fresh bamboo shoots and dash of red pepper. Stir to mix and continue to cook until completely heated through. Remove your mixture from heat.

5. Use a small sized saucepan and add in your water, vinegar, raw honey and favorite kind of soy sauce. Bring this mixture to a simmer over low heat and allow to cook for at least 2 minutes.

6. Mix together your cornstarch and water in a small sized bowl. Add to your honey mixture and stir to evenly incorporate. Continue cooking until your sauce is thick in consistency.

7. Remove from heat and pour over your vegetables and tofu. Toss to combine and serve with a garnish of your scallions.

Orange and Ginger Smothered Tofu Triangles

Here is yet another Asian inspired dish that I know you are going to want to make over and over again. This is not only an incredibly filling dish, but it is the perfect way to satisfy your strongest sweet tooth.

Makes: 4 Servings

Total Prep Time: 1 Hour and 25 Minutes

Ingredients:

- 1 Pound of Tofu, Firm
- 1 Cup of Orange Juice, Fresh
- ¼ Cup of Vinegar, Rice Variety
- 1/3 Cup of Soy Sauce, Your Favorite Kind
- 1/3 Cup of Oil, Canola Variety
- 4 tsp. of Oil, Sesame Variety
- 3 Cloves of Garlic, Minced
- 1 Tbsp. of Ginger Root, Fresh and Minced
- ¼ tsp. of Red Pepper Flakes
- 1 Green Onion, Cut Into Thin Strips
- ¼ Cup of Cilantro, Fresh and Roughly Chopped
- 2 Chile Peppers, Dried, Chipotle Variety and Optional

Directions:

1. First place your tofu on its side. Cut into thin slices and then cut into 8 equal sized triangles. Cover your triangles with a paper towels and place a heavy skillet over the top. Allow to sit for the next 30 minutes.

2. After this time use a medium sized bowl and add in your fresh orange juice, vinegar, favorite kind of soy sauce, canola and sesame oil, minced garlic, ginger and dash of red pepper flakes. Whisk thoroughly to combine.

3. Place your tofu into a large sized baking dish and cover with your freshly made marinade. Top off with your green onions, fresh cilantro and chipotle peppers if you are using them. Cover with a sheet of plastic wrap and allow to sit in your fridge to marinate for the next 30 minutes.

4. During this time preheat your oven to 350 degrees.

5. Pour off some of your marinade from your tofu. Place into your oven to bake for the next 40 to 45 minutes or until golden in color.

6. Remove from your oven and allow to cool slightly before serving.

Easy Tofu Sandwich Spread

This is going to be one of the most popular sandwiches to make among your vegetarian friends and family. Serving this spread within sandwiches or serve as an appetizer with crackers for dipping.

Makes: 4 Servings

Total Prep Time: 15 Minutes

Ingredients:

- 1 Pound of Tofu, Firm
- 1 Stalk of Celery, Fresh and Finely Chopped
- 1 Green Onion, Fresh and Finely Chopped
- ½ Cup of Mayonnaise, Your Favorite Kind
- 2 Tbsp. of Soy Sauce, Your Favorite Kind
- 1 Tbsp. of Lemon Juice, Fresh

Directions:

1. First drain your block of tofu and place into your freezer to freeze overnight. After this time thaw your tofu and cut into even sized quarters. Pat dry with a few paper towels.

2. Crumble your tofu into a medium sized bowl.

3. Add in your fresh celery and green onion.

4. Add in your favorite kind of mayonnaise, your favorite kind of soy sauce and fresh lemon juice. Stir well to combine and serve whenever you are ready.

Vegetarian Style Stuffed Peppers

If you are a huge fan of traditional stuffed peppers, then this is the perfect dish for you to make. Made with the perfect combination of brown rice, nuts and cranberries, this is the perfect dish to make whenever you need a little filling up.

Makes: 6 Servings

Total Prep Time: 1 Hour and 20 Minutes

Ingredients:

- 1 ½ Cups of Brown Rice
- 6 Bell Peppers, Green in Color and Large in Size
- 3 Tbsp. of Soy Sauce, Your Favorite Kind
- 3 Tbsp. of Sherry, Cooking Variety
- 1 tsp. of Worcestershire Sauce, Vegetarian Style
- 1 ½ Cups of Tofu, Extra Firm Variety
- ½ Cup of Cranberries, Dried and Sweet Variety
- ¼ Cup of Pecans, Finely Chopped
- ½ Cup of Parmesan Cheese, Freshly Grated
- Dash of Salt and Black Pepper, For Taste
- 2 Cups of Tomato Sauce
- 2 Tbsp. of Brown Sugar, Light and Packed

Directions:

1. The first thing that you will want to do is preheat your oven to 350 degrees. While your oven is heating up place a large sized saucepan over high heat. Add in three cups of water and allow to come to a boil. Add in your rice once boiling and reduce the heat to low. Cover your saucepan and allow to simmer for the next 40 minutes.

2. While your rice is cooking take your peppers and seed and core them. Make sure that you leave the bottoms intact. Transfer to a large sized microwave safe dish and add in at least half of water. Place into your microwave and cook on the highest setting for the next 6 minutes.

3. Then use a small sized frying pan and set over medium heat. Add in your soy sauce, wine and Worcestershire sauce. Stir to combine. Add in your tofu and allow to simmer until your liquid has been fully absorbed.

4. Add in your cooked rice, tofu, fresh cranberries, nuts, parmesan cheese, dash of salt and pepper. Stir thoroughly to combine and pack this mixture inside of your peppers.

5. Place your stuffed peppers into a large sized baking dish. Place into your oven to bake for the next 25 to 30 minutes or until the tops are light gold in color.

6. While your peppers are cooking use a small sized saucepan and place over low heat. Add in your tomato sauce and light brown sugar. Stir to combine and cook until piping hot. Spoon sauce over your peppers and serve right away.

Cheese and Tofu Stuffed Shells

If you are craving authentic Italian cuisine, then this is the perfect tofu dish for you to make. Packed full of tofu and covered in melted cheese, this is one dish I know you will want to make over and over again.

Makes: 4 Servings

Total Prep Time: 55 Minutes

Ingredients:

- 1, 16 Ounce Pack of Pasta Shells, Jumbo Variety
- 1/3 Cup of Carrot, Fresh and Grated
- ¼ Cup of Zucchini, Finely Shredded
- 3 Tbsp. of Onion, Finely Chopped
- 1, 8 Ounce Container of Tofu
- ½ Cup of Monterey Jack Cheese, Finely Shredded

- 1 Cup of Mozzarella Cheese, Finely Shredded and Evenly Divided
- ½ Cup of Ricotta Cheese, Soft
- 1 Egg White, Large in Size
- ½ tsp. of Salt, For Taste
- ½ tsp. of Pepper, For Taste
- 2, 8 Ounce Can of Tomatoes, Finely Diced
- 1/3 Cup of Tomato Paste
- 1 tsp. of Basil, Dried
- 1 tsp. of Oregano, Fresh and Dried
- ¼ tsp. of Garlic, Powdered Variety
- 1 tsp. of Garlic, Minced

Directions:

1. The first thing that you will want to do is preheat your oven to 350 degrees.

2. While your oven is heating up place a large sized pot of water over high heat. Bring the water to a boil. Season with a dash of salt and add in your pasta. Cook your pasta for at least 8 to 10 minutes or until tender to the touch. Drain after this time and set aside for later use.

3. While your pasta is cooking use a small sized saucepan and place over medium heat. Add in your grated carrots, fresh zucchini and onions. Stir to combine and pour in enough water to cover. Cook your veggies until tender to the touch. Once tender drain your veggies.

4. Next use a large sized bowl and add in your tofu. Mash your tofu thoroughly with a fork. Add in your carrot mixture, Monterey jack cheese, half a cup of your mozzarella cheese, soft ricotta, egg white and dash of salt and black pepper. Stir thoroughly until evenly mixed and set this mixture aside for later use.

5. Use a medium sized saucepan placed over medium to high heat and add in your fresh tomatoes, tomato paste, fresh basil, fresh oregano, powdered garlic and minced garlic. Stir to combine and bring this mixture to a boil. Once boiling reduce the heat to low and allow to simmer for the next 10 minutes.

6. Stuff each of your cooked pasta shells with at least one spoonful of your filling. Place each stuffed shell into a large sized baking dish. Pour your sauce over the top.

7. Place into your oven to bake for the next 25 minutes. After this time sprinkle your remaining mozzarella cheese and continue to bake for an additional 5 minutes or until melted.

9. Remove and allow to cool slightly before serving.

Simple Chocolate Tofu Pie

If you are a huge fan of chocolate, then this is one tofu recipe I know you are going to love making. It is creamy in consistency and great to satisfy those strong chocolate cravings.

Makes: 8 Servings

Total Prep Time: 40 Minutes

Ingredients:

- 1 Pound of Tofu, Silk Variety
- ½ Cup of Cocoa Powdered, Unsweetened Variety
- 1 Cup of Sugar, White in Color
- 1 Tbsp. of Vanilla, Pure
- ½ tsp. of Vinegar, Cider Variety
- 1, 9 Inch Graham Cracker Crust, Fully Prepared

Directions:

1. The first thing that you will want to do is to preheat your oven to 375 degrees.

2. While your oven is heating up place your tofu into a food processor. Blend on the highest setting until smooth in consistency.

3. Add in your powdered cocoa, white sugar, pure vanilla and cider vinegar. Stir thoroughly to combine and pour this mixture into your graham cracker crust.

4. Place into your oven to bake for the next 25 minutes.

5. After this time remove and place into your fridge to chill for the next hour. Serve whenever you are ready and enjoy.

Tofu Packed Stroganoff

Here is yet another great tasting tofu dish that you can make if you are a huge fan of beef stroganoff. Packed full of hearty tofu and mushroom, this is a dish the entire family will fall in love with.

Makes: 8 Servings

Total Prep Time: 45 Minutes

Ingredients:

- 1, 16 Ounce Pack of Egg Noodles, Uncooked Variety
- 2, 12 Ounce Pack of Tofu, Extra Firm Variety, Drained and Finely Diced
- 1 Tbsp. of Oil, Vegetable Variety
- 2 Onions, Thinly Sliced
- 1, 12 Ounce Container of Cottage Cheese, Soft to the Touch
- 2 Tbsp. of Sour Cream, Soft
- 1 Sprig of Dill Weed, Fresh and Roughly Chopped
- 8 Ounces of Mushrooms, Thinly Sliced
- 1 tsp. of Garlic, Minced
- 2 Tbsp. of Soy Sauce, Your Favorite Kind

Directions:

1. First bring a large sized pot of water to a boil over high heat. Once your water is boiling add in your egg noodles and cook for the next 8 to 10 minutes or until soft to the touch. Drain and set aside for later use.

2. Next heat up some oil in a large sized skillet placed over medium to high heat. Once your oil is hot enough add in your tofu and cook for at least 5 minutes on each side or until light brown in color. Set aside for later use.

3. Then add your onions into your skillet and cook until tender to the touch. Add in your mushrooms next along with your garlic and favorite kind of soy sauce. Stir to combine and continue to cook until piping hot.

4. Use a large sized bowl and add in your soft cottage cheese, soft sour cream and freshly chopped dill. Stir to combine and add this mixture to your skillet.

5. Return your tofu to your skillet and stir thoroughly to coat. Continue to cook until piping hot.

6. Remove from heat and serve over your cooked noodles. Enjoy right away.

Tofu Style Salad

This is a healthy and filling salad that any tofu lover will certainly enjoy. Packed full of tofu, fresh snow peas and savory ginger and garlic, this is the perfect dish to make whenever you are looking for something on the lighter side.

Makes: 4 Servings

Total Prep Time: 1 Hour and 20 Minutes

Ingredients:

- 1 Tbsp. of Chili Sauce, Sweet Variety
- ½ tsp. of Ginger Root, Freshly Grated
- 2 Cloves of Garlic, Crushed
- 1 Tbsp. of Soy Sauce, Dark in Color
- 1 Tbsp. of Oil, Sesame Variety
- ½, 16 Ounce Pack of Tofu, Firm, Drained and Finely Diced
- 1 Cup of Snow Peas, Fresh and Trimmed

- 2 Carrots, Small in Size and Freshly Grated
- 1 Cup of Red Cabbage, Fresh and Roughly Shredded
- 2 Tbsp. of Peanuts, Finely Chopped

Directions:

1. Use a large sized bowl and add in your chili sauce, ginger, minced garlic, favorite kind of soy sauce and sesame style oil. Stir thoroughly to combine.

2. Add your tofu into this mixture and cover with a sheet of plastic wrap. Allow to marinate for the next hour.

3. After this time bring a large sized pot filled with water to a boil over medium heat. Once your water is boiling add in your snow peas and allow to boil for the next 1 to 2 minutes. Immerse immediately in a bowl of cold water. Drain and add into a large sized bowl.

4. In this bowl add in your peas, fresh carrots, chopped cabbage and chopped peanuts. Add in your tofu with this marinate and toss to coat. Serve whenever you are ready.

Savory Tofu Vindaloo

Here is yet another great tasting vegetarian style tofu dish that you will fall in love with. Typically served in many Indian restaurants, this is a filling dish that pairs excellently with some basmati rice for the tastiest results.

Makes: 6 Servings

Total Prep Time: 1 Hour

Ingredients:

- 3 Tbsp. of Oil, Vegetable Variety
- 1, 2 Inch Piece of Ginger Root, Peeled and Minced
- 2 Onions, Cut Into Halves and Thinly Sliced
- ½ a Head of Cauliflower, Cut Into Small Sized Florets
- 3 Carrots, Fresh, Peeled and Thinly Sliced
- 3 Tbsp. of Curry Powder, Vindaloo Variety
- 6 Tbsp. of Tomato Paste
- 1, 15 Ounce Can of Milk, Coconut Variety
- 1 Cup of Broth, Vegetable Variety and Homemade Preferable
- 1, 15 Ounce Can of Beans, Garbanzo Variety, Drained and Rinsed
- 1 Pound of Tofu, Extra Firm and Cut Into Small Sized Cubes
- 1 Cup of Mushrooms, Thinly Sliced
- Dash of Salt, For Taste

Directions:

1. Heat up some oil in a large sized pot placed over medium to high heat. Once your oil is hot enough add in your ginger and cook until it become brown in color. This should take at least 2 minutes.

2. Then add in your onions, fresh cauliflower and fresh carrots. Continue to cook for the next 5 minutes or until soft to the touch.

3. Add in your curry powder and tomato pasta. Stir thoroughly until smooth in consistency.

4. Add in your coconut style milk, homemade vegetable broth and beans. Add in your tofu and mushrooms. Fold gently to combine and season with a dash of salt.

5. Bring this mixture to a simmer and reduce the heat to low or medium. Cover and allow your mixture to simmer until tender to the touch. This should take at least 15 minutes.

6. Remove from heat and serve right away.

Vegan Style Cheesecake

If you are looking for a vegan version of cheesecake, then this is the perfect recipe for you to put together. This delicious cheesecake is baked in a graham crack style pie and chilled until you are ready to serve it.

Makes: 6 Servings

Total Prep Time: 3 Hours and 20 Minutes

Ingredients:

- 1, 12 Ounce Pack of Tofu, Soft To The Touch
- ½ Cup of Milk, Soy Variety
- ½ Cup of Sugar, White in Color
- 1 Tbsp. of Vanilla, Pure
- ¼ Cup of Maple Syrup, Your Favorite Kind
- 1, 9 Inch Graham Cracker Crust

Directions:

1. The first thing that you will want to do is preheat your oven to 350 degrees.

2. While your oven is heating up place your tofu, soy style milk, white sugar, pure vanilla and favorite kind of maple syrup into a blender. Blend on the highest setting until smooth in consistency.

3. Pour this mixture into your pie crust.

4. Place into your oven to bake for the next 30 minutes. After this time remove from your oven and allow to cool before transferring into your fridge to chill completely. Serve whenever you are ready.

Savory Agedashi-esque Style Tofu

If you are a huge fan of Japanese recipes, then this is one tofu dish you need to try for yourself. For the tastiest results be sure to serve this dish with some stir fried rice or oriental meal.

Makes: 2 Servings

Total Prep Time: 15 Minutes

Ingredients:

- 1, 12 Ounce Pack of Tofu, Extra Firm Variety
- 3 Tbsp. of Cornstarch
- Some Oil, For Frying
- 2 Green Onions, Fresh and Roughly Chopped
- 2 Tbsp. of Hoisin Sauce

Directions:

1. First cut your tofu into 12 equal sized cubes.

2. Then place your cornstarch into a small sized bowl and dredge your tofu on each side or until thoroughly coated.

3. Heat up some oil in a large sized saucepan until piping hot. Add in your tofu and fry for the next 3 to 5 minutes or until crispy. Remove and drain on a plate lined with some paper towels.

4. Drizzle your hoisin sauce over the top and top off with your green onions. Serve right away and enjoy.

Tofu Packed Quiche with Broccoli

This is perhaps one of the best quiche recipes you will ever come across. Not only is it incredibly easy to make, but it is packed will some delicious and healthy broccoli that you will fall in love with.

Makes: 6 Servings

Total Prep Time: 1 Hour and 5 Minutes

Ingredients:

- 1, 9 Inch Pie Crust, Unbaked Variety
- 1 Pound of Broccoli, Fresh and Finely Chopped
- 1 Tbsp. of Olive Oil, Extra Virgin Variety
- 1 Onion, Large in Size and Finely Chopped
- 4 Cloves of Garlic, Minced
- 1 Pound of Tofu, Firm and Drained
- ½ Cup of Soy Milk
- ¼ tsp. of Mustard, Dijon Variety
- ¾ tsp. of Salt, For Taste
- ¼ tsp. of Nutmeg, Ground Variety
- ½ tsp. of Red Pepper, Ground and For Taste
- Dash of Black Pepper, For Taste
- 1 Tbsp. of Parsley, Fresh and Dried
- 1/8 Cup of Parmesan Cheese, Soy Variety

Directions:

1. Preheat your oven to 400 degrees. While your oven is heating up place your pie crust into your oven and bake for the next 10 to 12 minutes.

2. While your crust is baking place your fresh broccoli into a steam over at least one inch of boiling water. Cook until tender to the touch. This should take at least 2 to 6 minutes. Drain and set aside for later use.

3. Heat up some oil in a large sized skillet placed over medium to high heat. Once your oil is hot enough add in your onions and garlic and cook until golden in color. Add in your broccoli and stir thoroughly to combine.

4. Next use a blender and add in your firm tofu, soy milk, Dijon mustard, dash of salt and black pepper, red pepper, ground nutmeg, fresh parsley and soy style Parmesan cheese. Blend on the highest setting until smooth in consistency.

5. Add this mixture into a large sized bowl and add in your broccoli mixture. Stir to combine and pour into your pie crust.

6. Place into your oven to bake for the next 35 to 40 minutes or until your quiche is fully set. Remove and allow to sit for at least 5 minutes before serving.

Tofu Style Keema

If you have never heard of keema before, then this is one recipe you need to give a try. This dish is made with minced tofu, fresh green peas and served on top of a bed of rice for the tastiest results.

Makes: 4 Servings

Total Prep Time: 40 Minutes

Ingredients:

- 1, 16 Ounce Pack of Tofu, Firm To The Touch
- 3 Tbsp. of Oil, Vegetable Variety
- 1 tsp. of Cumin Seeds, Lightly Toasted
- 1 Onion, Finely Chopped
- 1 tsp. of Ginger Root, Freshly Minced
- 1 tsp. of Garlic, Minced
- 1 Cup of Peas, Frozen and Thawed
- 2 tsp. of Curry, Powdered Variety
- 1 Cup of Tomatoes, Fresh and Finely Chopped
- Dash of Salt, For Taste
- 1 Jalapeno Pepper, Fresh and Finely Chopped

Directions:

1. First place your tofu into a colander and cover with a plate. Add a heavy skillet over your tofu and allow to sit for the next 30 minutes or until somewhat drained. Place into your freezer after this time to freeze for the next 24 hours.

2. After this time remove your tofu from your freezer and defrost completely. Mince your tofu next and set aside for later use.

3. Heat up some oil in a large sized skillet placed over medium heat. Once your oil is hot enough add in your cumin seeds and cook until slightly brown in color.

4. Add in your onion, ginger and minced garlic. Cook for the next 5 minutes or until brown in color.

5. Add in your tofu, fresh peas and powdered curry. Continue to cook for the next 5 minutes before adding in your tomatoes and dash of salt. Stir to combine.

6. Cover and allow your mixture to cook for the next 15 minutes. After this time add in your pepper and continue to cook for another 2 to 3 minutes.

7. Remove from heat and serve right away.

Taiwanese Style Fried Tofu

This delicious tofu dish is one that can be served as a side dish or can be made as a tasty snack. For the tastiest results serve this dish with some rice and some of your favorite vegetables. Regardless I know you are going to love it.

Makes: 5 Servings

Total Prep Time: 30 Minutes

Ingredients:

- 1 Pack of Tofu, Extra Firm
- 1/3 Cup of Soy Sauce, Your Favorite Kind
- 2 tsp. of Vinegar, Black Variety and Chinese Style
- 1 tsp. of Oil, Sesame Variety
- 1 tsp. of Sugar, White in Color
- 3 Tbsp. of Olive Oil, Extra Virgin Variety

- 3 Cloves of Garlic, Minced
- ¼ Cup of Green Onions, Fresh and Finely Chopped
- Dash of Salt and Black Pepper, For Taste

Directions:

1. The first thing that you will want to do is cut your tofu in half. Slice into thick slices.

2. Then use a small sized bowl and add in your favorite kind of soy sauce, vinegar, sesame style oil and white sugar. Stir thoroughly to combine and set aside for later use.

3. Next heat up some olive oil in a large sized skillet placed over medium heat. Once your oil is hot enough add in your garlic and fresh green onions. Cook for the next 20 seconds before adding in your tofu. Cook until brown in color on all sides.

4. Pour in your sauce into your skillet and continue to cook until your sauce has been fully incorporated. This should take at least 2 to 3 minutes.

5. Remove from heat and season with a dash of salt and pepper. Enjoy right away.

Filling Tofu and Cauliflower Masala

This Indian inspired tofu dish is one that you will want to make over and over again. Savory cauliflower and tofu smothered in a hot masala sauce, this is one dish you will want to make whenever you are cravings something on the filling side.

Makes: 4 Servings

Total Prep Time: 1 Hour and 30 Minutes

Ingredients:

- 1, 16 Ounce Pack of Tofu, Firm
- ½ Cup of Yogurt, Plain
- 2 Tbsp. of Lemon Juice, Fresh
- 2 tsp. of Cumin, Ground Variety

- ½ tsp. of Cayenne Pepper, For Taste
- 1 tsp. of Paprika
- 1 tsp. of Garam Masala
- 1 Tbsp. of Ginger Root, Fresh and Minced
- 2 Tbsp. of Butter, Unsalted Variety
- 4 Cloves of Garlic, Minced
- 3 Serrano Peppers, Seeded and Minced
- 4 tsp. of Coriander, Ground Variety
- 2 tsp. of Cumin, ground Variety
- 2 tsp. of Garam Masala
- ½ tsp. of Salt, For Taste
- 1, 16 Ounce Can of Tomato Sauce
- 1 Head of Cauliflower, Fresh and Cut Into Small Sized Florets
- 2 Cups of Cream, Half and Half
- 1 Cup of Peas, Frozen
- ¼ Cup of Cilantro, Fresh and Roughly Chopped

Directions:

1. Place your tofu onto a place and place a skillet over the top. Allow to sit while being pressed for the next 20 to 30 minutes. Drain off the excess liquid.

2. After this time preheat your oven to 375 degrees. While your oven is heating up grease a large sized baking sheet.

3. Add your yogurt, fresh lemon juice, two spoonfuls of your cumin, dash of cayenne pepper, paprika, at least one teaspoon of your garam masala and minced ginger into a large sized bowl. Stir thoroughly to combine.

4. Cut your tofu into small sized cubes and add into your yogurt mixture. Toss to combine and place onto your baking sheet.

5. Place into your oven to bake for the next 45 minutes to an hour. Make sure you turn your tofu mixture every 15 minutes.

6. Melt your butter into a large sized skillet over medium heat. Once your butter is fully melted add in your garlic and pepper. Cook for the next 3 minutes or until soft to the touch.

7. Add in your ground coriander, ground cumin, garam masala and dash of salt. Stir to combine and cook for another minute. Then add in your tomato sauce and florets of cauliflower. Stir to combine and cover. Cook for the next 15 minutes or until tender to the touch.

8. Once your cauliflower is tender to the touch and add in your half and half, fresh peas, fresh cilantro and cubed tofu. Bring to a simmer and cook for the next 5 minutes or until thick in consistency.

Traditional Pad Thai Noodles

This authentic Thai recipe is one I know you are going to fall in love with. It is incredibly easy to make and is absolutely delicious, even the pickiest of eaters are going to love this dish.

Makes: 4 Servings

Total Prep Time: 2 Hours

Ingredients:

- 2/3 Cup of Vermicelli, Rice Variety and Dried
- ¼ Cup of Oil, Peanut Variety
- 2/3 Cup of Tofu, Sliced Thinly
- 1 Egg, Large in Size and Beaten Lightly
- 4 Cloves of Garlic, Chopped Finely
- ¼ Cup of Broth, Vegetable Variety
- 2 Tbsp. of Lime Juice, Fresh
- 2 Tbsp. of Soy Sauce, Your Favorite Kind
- 1 Tbsp. of Sugar, White in Color
- 1 tsp. of Salt, For Taste
- ½ tsp. of Red Chili Flakes, Dried Variety
- 3 Tbsp. of Peanuts, Finely Chopped
- 1 Pound of Bean Sprouts, Fresh and Evenly Divided
- 3 Green Onions, Thinly Sliced and Evenly Divided
- 3 Tbsp. of Peanuts, Finely Chopped
- 2 Limes, Fresh and For Garnish

Directions:

1. First place your noodles into a bowl and fill with some piping hot water. Allow to soak for the next 30 minutes to an hour. After this time drain and set aside for later use.

2. Next heat up some oil in a large sized wok and place over medium heat. Once your oil is hot enough add in your tofu and cook until golden brown in color on all sides. Once cooked remove and set on a plate lined with paper towels.

3. Add in some oil into your wok. Once it is hot enough add in your beaten egg and cook until thoroughly scrambled. Remove from your wok and set aside for later use.

4. Pour in some more oil into your wok. Once piping hot add in your garlic and drained noodles. Toss to thoroughly coat and add in your homemade broth, fresh lime juice, favorite kind of soy sauce and white sugar. Toss gently and push to the side of your wok.

5. Add in your tofu, scrambled egg, dash of salt, peanuts and chili flakes. Toss again to combine before adding in your bean sprouts and green onions. Continue to cook until slightly soft to the touch. This should take at least a minute or two.

6. Remove from heat and serve with a drizzle of your peanut oil. Garnish with your bean sprouts, green onions and lime wedges.

Tofu Style Turkey

If you are looking for a healthy and guilt free alternative for your average Thanksgiving style turkey, then this is the perfect dish for you. It is so delicious I know you will want to celebrate it every Thanksgiving.

Makes: 4 Servings

Total Prep Time: 3 Hours and 5 Minutes

Ingredients:

- 1 Pound of Tofu, Firm To The Touch
- 1 tsp. of Salt, For Taste
- ¼ tsp. of Marjoram, Dried Variety
- ¼ tsp. of Savory, Dried
- ¼ tsp. of Black Pepper, For Taste
- 1, 12 Ounce Pack of Bread Stuffing, Dried
- ¼ Cup of Margarine, Soy Variety
- 1 Slice of Bread, Cut Into Small Sized Cubes
- ½ tsp. of Sage
- 2 Tbsp. of Water, Warm
- 5 Tbsp. of Oil, Vegetable Variety and Evenly Divided
- 1 tsp. of Barbecue Sauce, Your Favorite Kind
- ½ tsp. of Mustard, Fully Prepared
- 1 Tbsp. of Jam, Orange Variety
- 1 tsp. of Orange Juice, Fresh
- 1 Tbsp. of Sesame Seeds, Lightly Toasted

Directions:

1. First drain and rinse your tofu. Then place into a food processor and blend on the highest setting until smooth in consistency.

2. Then add in your dash of salt, marjoram, dried savory and dash of pepper. Stir thoroughly to combine.

3. Place your tofu through a sieve and refrigerate after this time.

4. Meanwhile use a medium sized saucepan and place over medium to high heat. Add in your dried stuffing mix, at least 2/3 cup of water and your soy margarine. Stir to combine and bring this mixture to a boil. Once boiling reduce the heat to low and cover. Cook for the next 5 minutes. Remove from heat and then allow to stand for about 5-7 minutes before fluffing with a fork.

5. Add your bread cubes into your breadcrumb mixture along with your sage and at least two spoonfuls of your water.

6. After this time preheat your oven to 350 degrees. While your oven is heating up grease a large sized baking sheet with some oil.

7. Form a well in your tofu and spoon your stuffing mixture into it. Smooth the surface over with a spoon. Transfer to your baking sheet.

8. Place into your oven to bake for the next 30 minutes.

9. During this time make your glaze. To do this add your barbecue sauce, mustard, jam, fresh orange juice, toasted sesame seeds and at least three spoonfuls of your oil. Stir thoroughly to combine.

10. After 30 minutes of baking, brush your tofu with your glaze. Return back to your oven to bake for another 20 minutes.

11. After this time turn your oven to broil and allow your tofu to broil for at least 3 to 5 minutes or until brown in color and crispy to the touch.

12. Remove from your oven and allow to cool slightly before serving.

Tofu Fillet Sandwiches

If you are a vegetarian but you also won't eat fish, then this is the perfect dish for you to make. While this dish does not use fish, it is still as filling and delicious.

Makes: 4 Servings

Total Prep Time: 45 Minutes

Ingredients:

- 1, 12 Ounce Pack of Tofu, Firm, Drained and Sliced Into 4 Pieces
- 1 Cup of Bread Crumbs, Dried
- 1 tsp. of Kelp, Powdered Variety
- ¼ tsp. of Garlic, Powdered Variety
- ¼ tsp. of Paprika
- ¼ tsp. of Onion, Powdered Variety
- 1 tsp. of Salt, For Taste
- Some Olive Oil, Extra Virgin Variety
- Ingredients For Your Tartar Sauce:
- ½ Cup of Mayonnaise, Your Favorite Kind
- ¼ Cup of Relish, Dill Pickle Variety
- 1 Tbsp. of Lemon Juice, Fresh
- 4 Hamburger Buns, Whole Wheat Variety and Split Open

Directions:

1. The first thing that you are going to have to do is preheat your oven to 350 degrees.

2. While your oven is heating up use a large sized bowl and add in your dried bread crumbs, powdered kelp, powdered garlic, powdered onion, paprika and dash of salt. Stir thoroughly to combine.

3. Next dip your tofu slices in your olive oil. Then roll in your bread crumb mixture, making sure to coat thoroughly on all sides.

4. Place your tofu slices onto a baking sheet and place into your oven to bake for the next 30 minutes or until golden brown in color on all sides. Make sure that you turn during the baking process.

5. Next use a medium sized bowl and add in your favorite kind of mayonnaise, relish and fresh lemon juice. Stir thoroughly until evenly blended.

6. Brush each hamburger bun with your olive oil. Toast in your oven and top with your tartar sauce and baked tofu slices. Serve right away and enjoy.

Tofu Style Burgers

These tofu burgers are so delicious you won't want to eat regular burgers again. For the tastiest results serve these burgers with some fresh lettuce, onions, tomato slices and your favorite kind of mayonnaise.

Makes: 6 Servings

Total Prep Time: 3 Days

Ingredients:

- 1, 12 Ounce Pack of Tofu, Firm
- 2 tsp. of Oil, Vegetable Variety
- 1 Onion, Small in Size and Finely Chopped
- 1 Stalk of Celery, Finely Chopped
- 1 Egg, Large in Size and Beaten Lightly
- ¼ Cup of Cheddar Cheese, Finely Shredded
- Dash of Salt and Black Pepper, For Taste
- ½ Cup of Oil, Vegetable Variety

Directions:

1. First place your tofu into your freezer to freeze for at least 72 hours before use. Once you are ready take your tofu out of your freezer. Then fill up a large sized saucepan with a generous amount of water and bring to a simmer over medium heat. Add your tofu in the package into your water and allow to simmer for at least 20 minutes.

2. Next heat up some oil in a small sized skillet. Once your oil is hot enough add in your onions and fresh celery. Cook until soft to the touch. Transfer to a medium sized bowl and set aside for later use.

3. Once your tofu is fully thawed, make sure that you squeeze out the excess water. Then chop your tofu and place into a bowl with your onion mixture. Add in your egg, shredded cheese, and dash of salt and pepper. Stir thoroughly until combined.

4. Heat up a large sized skillet over medium to high heat. Add in your oil and once the oil is hot enough drop your tofu mixture into the hot oil and flatten with a spatula. Fry on both sides for at least 5 to 7 minutes or until golden in color.

5. Remove and drain on a plate lined with paper towels. Serve right away and enjoy.

Easy Braised Tofu

This is a dish that you can typically find in many Chinese restaurants and now with this recipe you can make it in the comfort of your own home. Feel free to add in a lot of vegetables for the tastiest results.

Makes: 4 Servings

Total Prep Time: 30 Minutes

Ingredients:

- 1, 14 Ounce Pack of Tofu, Firm To The Touch
- Some Cooking Spray
- 3 tsp. of Oil, Sesame Variety and Evenly Divided
- 1, 8 Ounce Can of Chestnuts, Water Variety and Drained

- 3 Ounces of Mushrooms, Shiitake Variety and with Stems Removed
- 1 ½ Cups of Snow Peas, Trimmed
- ½ tsp. of Sauce, Oyster Flavored
- 1 Cup of Water, Warm

Directions:

1. First slice a block of tofu into 3 long slabs. Then wrap each in some paper towels and squeeze out the excess water.

2. Next coat a large sized skillet with a generous amount of cooking spray. Add in your sesame oil and once your oil is hot enough add in your tofu slabs. Fry for at least 5 minutes on each side or until brown in color on all sides. Remove from your skillet and slice into small sized cubes.

3. Add in your remaining oil into your skillet and add in your drained chestnuts, shiitake mushrooms and snow peas. Stir to combine.

4. Mix together your warm water and sauce. Add into your skillet along with your fried tofu. Cover and reduce the heat to low. Allow to simmer for the next 10 minutes.

5. Remove from heat and serve whenever you are ready.

Stove Top Style Tofu Chili

Here is yet another filling dish you can make whenever you are looking to feel a little warmed up. Serve this with some crackers or bread for dipping and for the tastiest results.

Makes: 8 Servings

Total Prep Time: 1 Hour and 15 Minutes

Ingredients:

- 1/2, 12 Ounce Pack of Tofu, Extra Firm Variety
- 1 tsp. of Chili, Powdered Variety
- 1 Clove of Garlic, Minced
- 2 Tbsp. of Oil, Vegetable Variety
- ½ Cup of Onion, Finely Chopped
- 2 Stalks of Celery, Fresh and Finely Chopped
- ½ Cup of Corn, Whole Kernel Variety and Drained

- 1, 15.25 Ounce Can of Beans, Kidney Variety and Undrained
- 1, 14.5 Ounce Can of Tomatoes, Stewed Variety and Undrained
- 1 Quart of Water, Warm

Directions:

1. Use a medium sized bowl and add in your tofu. Crumble thoroughly with your hands and add in your powdered chili and minced garlic. Toss thoroughly to combine.

2. Heat up some oil in a large sized saucepan and place over medium heat. Once your oil is hot enough add in your onion and fresh celery. Cook until tender to the touch. Then add in your tofu mixture. Continue to cook for another 5 minutes.

3. Add in your whole kernel corn, beans and stewed style tomatoes. Add in your water and bring this mixture to a simmer.

4. Reduce the heat to low and allow to simmer for the next 50 minutes.

5. Remove from heat and serve while still piping hot.

Conclusion

Well, there you have it!

Hopefully by the end of this book you have learned why eating tofu can be one of the most beneficial things you can do for your body. I also hope that not only have you learned a few tips to cooking with tofu, but have also come across some of the most delicious tofu recipes that you won't find anywhere else.

So, what is next for you?

The next step for you to take is to begin making all of these delicious tofu recipes for yourself. Once you have done that it is time for you to try making your own authentic tofu recipes from scratch.

Good luck!

Author's Afterthoughts

Thank you for reading my book. Your feedback is important to us. It would be greatly appreciated if you could please take a moment to *REVIEW* this book on Amazon so that we could make our next version better

Thanks!

Martha Stone

Made in the USA
San Bernardino, CA
08 March 2019